17

UNDENIABLE TRAITS OF LEADERS IN CONSTRUCTION

Nicole Sanchez

Copyright © 2021 by Nicole Sanchez.

All rights reserved. This book or any portion thereof may not be reproduced or used in any manner whatsoever without the express written permission of the publisher except for the use of brief quotations in a book review.

This book is dedicated to my parents, Julie, Rich, and Nancy,
who poured into me and loved me so I could learn
to love and inspire others.

To my amazing daughter who is the light of my soul
and to my husband, who shows me what is possible.

TABLE OF CONTENTS

INTRODUCTION 1
1 | COURAGE 5
2 | COMPASSION 13
3 | ADAPTABLE 19
4 | PREPARED 25
5 | TRUSTWORTHY 31
6 | RELENTLESS 39
7 | UPPER-LEVEL MINDSET 45
8 | HUMILITY 51
9 | PATIENCE 59
10 | VISION 65
11 | IN ACTION 71
12 | DECISIVE 77
13 | FUN 83
14 | EFFECTIVELY COMMUNICATE 89
15 | EMPOWER 97
16 | CONFIDENCE 103
17 | SELF-AWARE 111
CONCLUSION 119
ABOUT THE AUTHOR 121

INTRODUCTION

"The key to successful leadership is influence, not authority."
- Kenneth H. Blanchard

Undoubtedly, the construction industry is one of the riskiest, most diverse, most expensive, and technically demanding industries globally. Due to its rapidly evolving and corporate structure, we have experienced dramatic changes over the past few decades. The industry is evolving with several innovative technologies and digitized materials being integrated to facilitate the speed at little or no cost in estimating and managing projects.

While labor costs are reduced due to these technological advancements, we often fail to adequately address one of our industry's most critical aspects: **leadership** at all project levels. For every project commissioned, many professionals and building contractors are involved, and to ensure success, we need an individual to keep everyone together. Without this leadership, failure is bound to occur.

Effective leaders do not lead from above but from within the team to ensure that a building is erected and a team is created despite challenges. As construction professionals, this shows us that, irrespective of whatever advancements or technologies are being used, labor has the most significant impact on any project. Without strategic, genuine, team-focused, and moral leaders to complement technology-driven and tool-based projects, failure is inevitable.

More than anything else, success in this industry is hinged on leaders' abilities to influence, motivate, and direct the available workforce to coordinate productivity. It is essential to identify technically proficient individuals, excellent communicators, effective managers, and good leaders. Finding the right team ensures budget and deadlines are met. Simultaneously, they will ensure collaboration, teamwork, and cooperation as projects are executed successfully.

As leaders, we recognize the human element. Since we are all unique, there are challenges, roadblocks, and conflicts, especially if a team member has underlying interests. However, great leaders utilize all available resources to ensure conflicts are averted challenges are sorted out.

Leadership in this industry is more about influencing team members rather than attempting to control them. Just like John C. Maxwell once stated, "As a leader, you must not only be out in front but also have your team members intentionally coming behind and acting on your vision without coercion."

Thus, it's not enough to lead, having just titles and roles stuck to your door or desk. It's more about gaining skills that influence and inspire team members into action. Having these traits encourage them to develop their ideas and solutions to become more productive and engaged in the project. Because of the interdisciplinary nature of construction jobs and the fact that team members may work for several different companies, there's an enormous need for leaders that can influence people to collaborate on the job.

INTRODUCTION

Not only that, leaders are supposed to create a working environment that elicits trust, openness, communication, and empowerment while being flexible and efficient to ensure project success. It isn't about hiring the best team of professionals. It's more about hiring a leader that ensures collaboration and empowerment among them. That isn't possible if such an individual hasn't built him/herself over time to become who they want their team members to be.

Everyone would like to be a great leader, someone who is well-liked and respected. However, several undeniable qualities are needed to successfully lead a team to execute leadership projects in the construction industry. Effective leadership in the industry is a combination of cognitive characteristics that begin from within first. It includes self-awareness, self-management, and social awareness. Having these first enables us, as leaders, to empower individuals, build teams, align and influence workers from different companies towards common goals, and manage such relationships. So, it begins with us, not with our team!

Every chapter of this book outlines and explains, in detail, these undeniable traits of successful leaders in the industry. This book serves to give directions on the several ways you can influence a team to follow your lead without coming off as "bossy" or unapproachable. These traits will always dictate the working atmosphere, so it's wise to learn how to balance them to achieve maximum productivity.

1 | COURAGE

"What separates effective leaders from ineffective leaders is the art of being courageous. So, it's not about fear; it will always be there. It's about what you do in the face of fear."

Fear, especially fear of failure, can be overwhelming and paralyzing. It keeps us from doing what we know is in the best interest of everyone involved, and it has been instilled in us over time, starting from childhood. We have always been told not to do certain things since childhood: pass the test, or you will fail the course, do this, or you will face the consequences. It continues as we mature, and it gradually strips away our natural courage to face ridicule or shame.

Everyone has this tendency. Sometimes, you know what you're doing, but in the next minute, something comes along that scares the living daylights out of you.

Well, you are not alone.

People who aren't afraid to fail and are brave in the face of risks, threats, and sudden change aren't superhuman. They are humans just like everyone else, but over time, they have learned to manage fear and put a foot forward, irrespective of the uncertainties.

All successful leaders and entrepreneurs are also fearful. What separates effective leaders from ineffective leaders is the art of being **courageous**. So, it's not about fear; it will always be there. It's about what you do in the face of fear.

Life is filled with risks, and fear is an essential factor in the construction industry. A leader's ability to master fear and be courageous determines their influence on those they lead during project execution. Leaders will only influence and effectively motivate their team to execute a project if they have built the mental and moral strength and will to persevere and withstand anything, on and off-site.

While bringing a team of highly skilled professionals into your boat, take courage along because it is what will keep you all from holding onto the boat when the storms arise. Courage is the core and foundation of the project's success and a metric for the leader you will turn out to be. It builds your influence on the team since they will trust your decisions. No one will follow, trust, or listen to a leader who doubts and worries over his or her choices, and if you find yourself doing this, you should reconsider leading that project.

In our industry today, risk is a necessary factor for innovation and success. As we evolve, effective leaders take chances by trying out dynamic new materials, robotic cranes, automatic builders, etc. on building complex structures, and as a leader, you'll need the courage to do so. With courage comes the willingness to try new things and fail in the pursuit of success.

Fear doesn't have to be your enemy, and failure should be seen positively as learning and growth. Despite the risks, you need to push forward with reckless abandon and do things that take you out of your comfort zone.

We all avoid holding ourselves accountable because we fear the outcome and responses from others. With courage, you feel the fear, but you still forge ahead anyway because it is the right thing to do. Great leaders master the fear over time, hold themselves accountable, not being afraid to take risks, make decisions, and work their way through conflicts, confrontations, and issues with team members. When leaders are filled with fear, doubts, or insecurity, they end up debilitating the team's ability to function and compromise strategic thinking, decision making, and productivity.

With courage, leaders can have a healthy and productive conversation since they will be more likely to stand up and speak openly and with conviction, challenge ideas and unacceptable behavior or activity, take responsibility, provide the team with positive and constructive feedback regularly, and engage in necessary conversations to solve build problems.

As a leader, you have to be willing to climb over obstacles, do what's complicated, and keep doing that every day. Fear is uncomfortable. Be able to push through awkward situations and be willing to make difficult decisions and not back down when things get complicated. Be courageous to put in new practices when working on a project. The leader's courage has a way of affecting everyone on-site, giving them the confidence needed to support the implementation of such practices on-site, thereby achieving extremely high levels of reliability throughout the project. Regardless of the challenges, discouragement, and setbacks, the team can persevere once they feel a leader's courage.

Practical Steps

Are you courageous enough already?
If not, then try the following:

- Understand that failure isn't the end, but rather a means to succeed again. When you fail to accomplish a task linked to a project, you just found another way to do it better than the way you started.

- Visualize yourself as unafraid. It will help you feed your mind with positive mental pictures of yourself performing at your best, enhancing confidence and competence in your performance.

- Practice having the courage you desire. It should be portrayed in your body postures: stand up straight, smile, move quickly and confidently, completely unafraid in a particular situation.

- Find out how you get motivated and feed on it to harness your full potential. If other leaders, be it in the construction industry or not, motivate you, then surround yourself with them.

- Recognize your fear. Constantly probe yourself on what you are afraid of: the fear of project failure? Fear of being vulnerable? Fear of being criticized? Whichever one it is, recognizing it will help you focus on ways to avoid it and overcome it. Admit your fears, especially if you do not have answers. Saying, "I do not know," isn't a sign of weakness; instead, you are willing and open to your team's suggestions.

- Confront your fears immediately. After recognizing your fears, confront and deal headlong with them by addressing them. You can also get help in confronting and resolving it. When you do this, your self-esteem goes up, and your self-respect increases.

- Move toward the fear. Fear, the more you move towards it, the more it becomes an illusion, and the more your confidence increases. The more you feed it by backing away from it, the more it grows, dominating your thinking and feeling, preoccupying your thoughts all the time.

- Trust your instinct. Don't sideline your guts. Although emotions aren't needed when executing, listen to yourself, not your fear. It will be possible if you've built an intense mental character over time. Invest in your mental life; you need to know before you can trust what you know.

- Stay guided by your goals. Discuss with the team and collaborate on setting goals before undertaking projects. Set achievable goals; if your goals are low, you lack self-confidence and are scared of achieving standard benchmarks. If these goals are too high, you are only trying to mask your insecurities because no one can achieve them, knowing no one will criticize you. Set goals with achievable benchmarks, and then create plans to achieve them. The drive to meet the goals will exceed whatever fear you may have.

Remember, you are human and are likely to make mistakes. Don't dwell on them. Instead, see it as a learning process. Don't be shy or scared to ask for help or advice when necessary. When working on new projects, work with ideas that sound strange initially, experiment with new approaches, and assess the possible outcomes.

Adopt a growth mindset. It's not about being perfect every step of the way. No one is ever perfect all the time. Rather, it is about getting comfortable with the unknown and continuing anyway. Accept the possibility of failing and move on.

So, you are trying a new resource or material on a project for the first time?

Take courage. You might fail, or get it wrong, or you might do something absolutely incredible.

2 | COMPASSION

"Everyone loves love, and your team members aren't an exception. Show it and see yourself gaining several loyal individuals and long-lasting relationships."

Everyone within the team plays a distinct role, but achieving the goal comes from their collective efforts. Leaders have to ensure that team members are inspired so their performance can be in perfect harmony to achieve that outcome. The ability to inspire and keep team members engaged stems from having the grit to show you care! Only then will the team be truly excited enough about the work they're doing. When individuals perceive their contributions and ideas are valued and essential for delivering outcomes and continuous improvements to projects, success is assured.

Team engagement revolves around showing compassion, which, of course, doesn't cost a fortune. A great leader shows compassion through actions of love, laughter, and a listening ear.

Leaders can express love to team members by showing empathy under challenging situations, such as genuine understanding and sharing of feelings. Leaders show sympathy and a willingness to provide each team member with the support they need. Everyone loves love, and as a leader, your team members are no exception. Show it and see yourself gaining several loyal individuals and long-lasting relationships.

Also, compassionate leaders actively listen when facilitating an open dialogue among team members. They listen to each person's moods, emotions, and thoughts, not just the words. As these relationships progress, leaders will build respect and foster a culture of engagement. Additionally, this will help create a team that will form and implement successful strategies with impressive results. As a compassionate leader, your team won't be afraid to speak their minds while allowing for a candid discussion.

Beneath the debris, building equipment, and spreadsheets is a team of individuals with emotions. These are not robots made of iron. In the midst of the strenuous activity or challenge, a compassionate leader is able to lighten the mood! Work hard and play even harder.

Laugh! It isn't unprofessional; it humanizes you as a leader and puts the team at ease, making them enjoy the work they do. It flattens the hierarchy and creates equality. Leaders need to value team members as humans, not just as tools for finishing projects. People have to be led, not managed like tasks. It is not always about the projects commissioned and erected; it's all about care, not just in words but actions.

Compassionate leaders don't get all bossy. No one likes that. Instead, leaders inspire their team and create a culture of engagement through their conduct and actions towards them as humans, not by reinforcing authority. Such empathic actions make a difference and serve as a solid foundation for the team's successes and their abilities to bounce back from failures. When a great leader readily cares about the team's needs, listen to what they have to say, and enjoy working alongside them, they exhibit the same loyalty and respect their leadership has shown them in return.

An aura of safety, void of any toxicity, enables the entire team to show up with their concerns and vulnerability and fully be themselves. It makes them more motivated, creative, happy, and productive, especially if they know you've got their back at all times. Even the smallest amounts of care helps create trust and encourage them stay productive, put in collective efforts, and go the extra mile to support the projects' execution.

Practical Steps

Next time you are heading to a site or meeting with the office team, try the following:

- Be available and ready to listen. Set aside or scheduled a time each week for meetings where you can converse and interact without distractions with team members. If you are going to be available, be 100% physically, mentally, and emotionally open.

- Keep communication open, genuine, transparent, and back up your words with tangible actions. When conversing, empathically put yourself in the other person's shoes and understand their emotions and the message being passed. Ask open-ended questions and reflect on the feelings and words so they feel as though you are connecting with what they are saying. Observe the emotional cues from team members and be considerate of the other person's emotional state.

- Take time to understand individual styles and preferences when communicating with your team. For example, consider how each member communicates best; it could be through face-to-face meetings or voice calls. Know this before conveying your message while following their style of communication. It results in a loyal team that's committed to the mission of the team.

- Keep your emotions in check. You need not get upset or angry every time you receive insufficient information; when you do, they will quickly stop coming to you. Create a positive atmosphere so your team members can feel comfortable bringing you all types of information.

- Besides work, show genuine interest in their lives and interests. Know your team members individually. Although you're on-site, it does not mean that the only conversations you engage in should be about work. Find out what is most important to such an individual, what they love and are grateful for.

- Ask for information on birthdays, best hangouts, and names of loved ones. Make an effort to learn something new about the person. Since these things are personal, putting effort into knowing and doing them will create an emotional connection and engagement.

- Avoid autocratic leadership. Be tolerant and show careful thought and behavior to team members. Use your influence and authority to improve mutual respect and non-toxic working conditions.

- In making plans, consult team members to get more ideas or better suggestions. Discuss with them before springing ideas on them. Ask their thoughts on materials to be used in building; listen attentively to them, and value their suggestions.

- Value diversity by actively recognizing and appreciating each individual's perspectives, effort, results, potential, and experience. Additionally, provide regular and positive feedback on accomplished projects. Give credit to members that deserve it and showcase member's strength; it doesn't reduce your position.

- Ask for feedback from your team regarding their individual assigned role on the project. If the team isn't cool with the procedures, a discussion could improve or suggest other ways. When you encourage team members to identify problems and solve them, you will foster creative participation.

- Encourage cooperation by enabling your team to feed off each other's ideas and know each other's pressures and priorities. They can collaborate in providing a unified delivery, incredibly when resources are limited, or there is a risk the ideas might not work.

All of these can look overwhelming, but it's worth it. So, stretch out of your comfort zone, start small, and learn as you go. It will make all the difference!

3 | ADAPTABLE

"If the play isn't working, CHANGE THE PLAY."
- Joe Martino, COO Uprite Construction

Change is inevitable, and not everyone is comfortable with it. But amid changes, advancement, and transformation that comes with this digital age, some of us tend to resign to it despite its benefits. This occurs because we've become too attached to the same thing, and when it doesn't work anymore, it is hard for us to let go of it.

Undoubtedly, strong leadership is perceived as being decisive, persistent, and unwavering. Despite the focus, if one isn't flexible enough and ready to change course, failure becomes more likely to occur.

One undeniable trait of great leaders is knowing when they feel like a silly hamster in a wheel, running and running without results. These leaders know when the play isn't working anymore, and they aren't afraid to make a shift, embrace change, and stay relevant on course.

Change is bittersweet, but great leaders are not afraid to move from plan B to C, D to Z, and not feel stuck in a rut or feel like they have failed. Because they understand what failure is, they aren't bothered or ashamed to pivot and succeed after several failed approaches to executing a project. They've got guts because sticking to the old way is mediocre and the easy way out. They are more prepared to persevere when the pain of change starts popping up.

Pivoting is not a change in the overall goal but rather in the strategy used. With the rise of digitalization, robotics, and continuous technological advancement, pivoting is essential for success in the ever-evolving construction industry. Leaders in the industry aren't scared to shift and embrace anything that will catalyze change.

The more rapidly you pivot, the more effectively you'll remain in the game – a game for which the playbook keeps changing alongside changes in the way the construction industry operates.

Adaptable leaders know that there is no time to keep waiting and hoping, resisting change because everything is moving fast. These shifts can never return to their previous positions. Thus, to be successful, great leaders are strong enough to take charge and embrace the opportunity to pivot and lean into it with swiftness.

Often, these leaders are generally more concerned with how they persuade and influence team members to execute projects; however, being persuasive isn't just for your team members but also for you.

Are you also persuaded to take that "change?"

It all begins with the mind. Presently, one competitive advantage that we all need is a flexible mind that can change and adjust in the face of new technologies, new information, and new strategies.

The Mind

Demand for the construction of top-notch projects is high. Thus, residential and commercial structures continue to become more complex in execution, and as a leader, you need to make wise decisions to meet this demand. Being persuadable allows you to utilize technologies and data made available to make sure the most precise judgments are made and your team can execute top-notch structures, even if it contradicts what you previously believed would work.

Most leaders who stick to old approaches and procedures are static in thinking. Adaptable leaders change things when they are flexible mentally. When they incorporate into their thinking the concept of the new reality, accepting significant change in the form of the digital revolution, the advancements in robotics and AI, along with other new technologies, will be accessible.

With a rapidly evolving approach towards work, successful leaders in the industry have become more open to new ideas and fresh thinking, which is beneficial to the team and project success. In our fast-paced industry, we need to envision change and advancement. We try to initiate it first, and if it works, we control it. It is the best kind of change because it creates more opportunities, transforms the team, and ignites growth.

With our minds developed, we begin to think expansively about the future and what change might be a game-changer for the industry. Such change will deliver projects with better efficiency and results when we are brave enough to execute it. These leaders understand that trying out the "change" is never a loss. The world is changing faster than ever, and any given leader's willingness to change their mind is vital!

Perspectives

Leaders who pivot have also shifted in perspective. A frequent and better standpoint around change positively influences actions towards opportunities and project outcomes.

For instance, a change in perception towards site hazards will open their minds to leverage technology to reduce worker injury and improve worker health while increasing productivity. A shift in perspective can transform the opportunities you see as a leader, reignite waned motivation, and help you achieve more with the team.

Values

In pivoting, successful construction leaders do not throw off their core values. With their core values always in mind, their drive, daily thoughts, and actions are always aligned; hence decision-making is more effortless.

Apart from adapting to change, the speed at which we adapt to change is also essential. Things are changing in the industry; many are still holding onto the status quo, waiting too long to change their minds. Those who aggressively lean into those changes capitalize on them and continue thriving rather than struggling to catch up later.

The industry is becoming more competitive than ever with globalization and the rise of the internet. As such, leaders need to continually improve their skills and abilities and embrace feedback, no matter how uncomfortable. These criticisms would enable you to improve at a more rapid pace than others.

Often, society has pegged a notion that when people change their minds on something, they appear weak and flimsy, but this is not true. When change is the right thing to do, you need to go for it unapologetically. Sell it to your team and be clear on why you are changing your mind on something.

Get feedback, weigh decisions, and execute!

Practical Steps

Envision how you can pivot a project's strategies and activities in response to the changes while staying connected to your work's vital foundations:

- What would a successful pivot look like?

- What will define success for you in the next quarter?

- How would you and the team change your mental capacities to a point where new results become achievable?

Be sure to discuss these things with your team with an open mind.

4 | PREPARED

"You prepare yourself so that if a door opens up you are ready to take that opportunity. When the opportunity presents itself, you are either ready or you are not."
- Michael Boomsma, Cordoba Corp.

We are well aware that the ever-increasing demands for infrastructure require that we evolve as leaders. Evolution is impossible without better preparation; preparation is key to leveraging opportunities and evolution. It demands accountability and responsibility. Often, when we fail as leaders, it's perceived to be our lack of preparation. When an opportunity is missed, it is because we usually don't prepare ourselves well enough to see and seize it.

Therefore, one of the undeniable traits of leaders in the industry is knowing the short- and long-term preparation demands for successful project execution. Given proper timing and depth of a plan, if a leader falls short in their ability to prepare, the project's negative implications will become quickly apparent.

Successful leaders in the industry are always ready to leverage opportunities that arise, earnestly expectant for the next promotion. It also goes beyond the leader! These leaders know that they need to ensure their team members and the organization they serve are constantly evolving in a positive direction.

Practical Steps

To effectively prepare and be readily available for the next opportunity, we as leaders need to act on the following:

Think Strategically

We are more likely to tactically use their minds in envisioning the next phase of an opportunity by proactively planning to ensure that they act effectively despite any future challenge that might arise when the opportunity comes.

They prepare by asking themselves and their teams questions like:

- "If this happens, who am I going to be working with?"
- "What challenges are likely to arise?"
- "How can I best execute the project?"
- "'Is the resource readily available or not?"

Never Stop Being Accountable

Preparation is mostly about being proactive to deliver on a responsibility they are accountable for, and hence, as leaders, we should never cease being accountable to ourselves and others.

We should try to meet the deadline, pay attention to detail, ask the right questions, etc. This level of concern enables us to rise beyond inefficiencies and become much more accountable.

Improve Approach to Problem-Solving and Decision Making

We shouldn't be scared to put in the time and efforts toward owning skill-sets and capabilities to improve their problem-solving approach and become better decision-makers. When problems come to the surface, we should be prepared to solve these problems proactively and efficiently, not to lose time and financial resources put into the project; hence, we should learn how to use their strengths to prepare themselves better.

Failure Becomes a Guide

Often, preparation doesn't guarantee success, but a lack of preparation can certainly increase a project's chances of failure. To be great leaders, we should have an in-depth understanding that if a project fails in execution, it's because we haven't found the right way out. As such, failure becomes our guide to success.

Failure should activate our drive to become more diligent about our overall approach to better preparation. As a prepared leader, you become mindful of why things worked and why they didn't rather than give up everything. We need to value what we've learned from failed attempts by preparing with the same attention to detail to avoid mistakes or failures from happening again.

Embrace a New Start

Leaders must be prepared to change the play at the last second, especially when things change by the minute. As we plan for the future, we should plan for several scenarios. Although the goal remains the same, the strategies change to account for the unknowns. We must understand that some uncertainties and crises can arise at any given point. So, when projects don't go as planned, we should embrace a fresh start, becoming more innovative by looking for insights and building from where we are now to creating what could be instead of mourning over what was.

Let's become mentally prepared to adopt these new strategies, show off inspiration to an anxious and frustrated team, and set the tone that drives engagement.

Preparation Demands Credibility

As leaders, we often demand high performance from our team members to leverage opportunities, but most of the time, our team flops because we, ourselves, aren't prepared to lead them to it effectively. If a leader is not prepared to deliver the leadership their team members expect, then they ought not to expect them to perform.

When more is demanded from the team, the pressure to perform increases, and so does the pressure to lead them right.

Thus, we need to increase our performance standards for ourselves and, after that, the team we lead; and as such, preparation becomes a leading measure of success.

Take Time to Pause and Pay Attention

Although they move and think quickly, successful leaders take time to pause and pay closer attention to their team members. These leaders prepare themselves to lead more effectively and become poised to take advantage of opportunities by knowing what is happening with their team members.

As well-prepared leaders, we know we can't move forward if the team members are dysfunctional and broken, so we must broaden our observations of the team's state of mind and provide additional support, better resources, and the tools needed to succeed.

In becoming more aware of their needs, which they sometimes might not mention to you, you'd help prepare them effectively to be ready and available for opportunities.

Listen Carefully

These leaders prepare much better and intently when they listen to their team members. In listening to team members, you lead, prepare, and solve things that you otherwise couldn't if you only listen to yourself. So, endeavor always to ask questions and solicit your team's input as they share perspectives and opinions regarding the project. We should properly prepare ourselves with combined thoughts and recommendations, which will guide the project's objectives and desired outcomes.

5 | TRUSTWORTHY

"Stay true to your word. Construction is a small industry. It is so important that you stay consistent, and you do the right thing."
- Karl Krueziger, President, CW Driver

Another undeniable trait of successful leaders in the construction industry is the quality of being worthy of belief and trust. Credibility is one of the defining characteristics of effective leaders in the industry over long periods. It flows from character and competence built over time, and just like the other traits mentioned in the earlier chapters of this book, it is an asset to exceptional delivery of leadership.

More than ever, the industry needs credible leaders worthy of belief and trust because they turn out to be highly dependable in terms of expertise, information, decision-making, and creating win-win situations for all. The entire operations of a building project are coordinated around the tactical plan's timely execution; thus, unfulfilled promises, no matter how small, become critical in implementing those plans.

Over time, we should put in efforts in behaving in ways that cause people to see us as credible. To lead effectively, we must be believed and trusted, both in what we say and generally as an individual.

These behaviors include:

Consistency

Leaders that are consistent in their words and behaviors are reliable. Because of their consistency in not constantly shifting courses and reversing their decisions, they are relatively predictable and easy to work with. Team members watch leaders closely and look for how they behave according to their expressed values. If a leader can't practice what they preach or follow through on promises, they've lost the team's loyalty. As leaders, what we do each and every day is far more important than what we do just every now and again.

Honesty

Successful leaders are straightforward and honest, and they continuously work towards remaining true to themselves and the team they lead, having no hidden agendas and watching out for others' interests. Because of their transparency, they foster an open environment of respect and loyalty, where productivity is guaranteed and unethical behavior isn't tolerated.

Communication

Finally, these leaders connect and communicate with their team. It's clear that team members love to interact face-to-face to thrash out issues, but if you end up sending an email instead of a face-to-face time out, that won't turn out okay. As compared to a relatively non-responsive leadership style, loyalty and trustworthiness are built through effective interpersonal communication.

A team that perceives its leader to have low credibility is significantly more likely to criticize that leadership privately and laugh with them in public. They can never be loyal to a leader or execute jobs if not carefully watched because they don't believe them and their words. Since their word means nothing to them, they won't honor the leader's commitments and, hence, won't be trusted anymore, no matter how good they are at delivering results.

Credibility isn't a one-time thing but a process that is built over time. It involves time, effort, and patience, but it's worth investing in. Commitments are as small as setting meeting times and sticking to the time commitment. If leaders have formed the habit of canceling or rescheduling meetings for whatever reasons, they gradually lose trust. As a leader, behavior impacts how your team members view you. Thus, it would help if you were not out of touch with your behavior. If you behave wrongly, accept you made a mistake, make prompt amendments, and take full responsibility for your actions and decisions. You can communicate by admitting and apologizing about it and then putting your apology into action. Otherwise, team members won't take you seriously. As a trustworthy leader, you do not focus on your team's nonchalance because you caused it; instead, the attention should go to yourself. Openly criticize your behavior and actions to begin the process of rebuilding trust.

If you want your team members to be more accountable, start with yourself. Be more accountable, and they'll adopt your actions over time.

When you walk your talk, you lead by example, and you make your actions speak louder than your words. It makes you look more assertive and more authentic as there's a guarantee that you'd deliver that which you've promised since such trust will enable them to work with you much more efficiently and productively. Generally, you'd be seen as an asset, a valuable team player, and someone everyone wants to work with.

Successful leaders in the industry also recognize the importance of ongoing education to help them achieve what is required; hence, they continuously engage in learning processes to expand their knowledge. With such knowledge, they become competent at developing multiple solutions to problems.

Practical Steps

Here are potential ways to strengthen your credibility and dependability with a build project team:

- **Be more self-aware and intentional.** Monitor your words and be fully conscious of what you are promising. Ensure that your words become as essential to you as you want them to be to others!

- **Be organized.** We hastily agree to do things that get forgotten and drop off the radar. To prevent that, write down commitments immediately and assign a completion date to them.

- **Deliver results.** To gain credibility, you need to be results-oriented.

- **Be transparent.** Your team members watch you constantly, so you've got to be straight with them. Be upfront and transparent about what you are committing to do. Avoid lousy commitments that you should never have agreed to, as this can prove costly to your reputation.

- **Don't make promises you can't keep.** Know what you can change and what can't you before you commit; you might commit to things beyond your control or influence. So rather than act nice and fail, say no!

- **Ask for help.** Successful leaders aren't afraid to ask their team for support and assistance, especially if you can't keep commitments.

- **Demonstrate courage and resilience when working under pressure.** Remember, your team members often watch you. Do not allow challenges onsite or offsite to dictate your behavior negatively. Be positive by making most of the situation as you navigate the unknown.

- **Talk!** Communicate with everyone relevant to the project to avoid surprises and remove ambiguity. Provide feedback and honor the timelines.

Now take a test and keep track of how well you currently own your promises.

Building Credibility: A Quiz

1. Do you do what you say?

2. Are your words good enough?

3. Do you keep promises, agreements, and commitments?

4. Do you often claim you were misunderstood?

5. Do you know your stuff and what you don't know?

6. Are you open to suggestions from employees and co-workers?

7. Are you always right?

8. How do you respond when challenged or when someone questions your decision-making abilities?

9. Do you blame others when things go wrong but take the credit when things go right?

10. Do you change your story often?

11. Do you use justification?

12. Are you willing to take responsibility when a team member fails to deliver against expectations?

13. Do you dodge direct questions?

Regardless of your position, reliability is the cornerstone of your reputation. Keep your word; others are counting on it. Your team plans their work, operations, schedule, hopes, and expectations on what you've promised. Don't shatter that trust they have in you; your influence and trust will drop like a rock, and honor is at stake.

6 | RELENTLESS

"These are leaders with grit and guts, having the tenacity and fortitude to pursue regardless of the unknown."

Another trait that separates great leaders in the industry from others is that they have a never-say-never attitude. Problems and challenges are a part of any project. Still, with this trait, you can confront these challenges consistently, assess their severity, seek new solutions, and retain perspective to keep the team on track.

Executing projects isn't just about the plans, team, or resources available; it also has to do with being relentless, persevering through whatever challenges might arise during project executions, and developing the ability to weather brutal storms.

Being relentless requires several doses of determination, hard work, and a mindset to move forward, look for solutions, and work toward success. No one wants to follow a leader who relents or cowers in the face of challenges; thus, being relentless is a crucial driving trait behind strong leadership.

These leaders see failure as a temporary obstacle, and hence, they do not abandon projects due to a lack of enough resources or relax when things go their way. They remain unyielding and unbending, never-ceasing, yet tenacious and determined. They do not give up in the face of constraint; instead, they always dream up creative ways to work around challenging problems. Nothing gets in their way! They will give all their time and efforts to see the end of a project: not giving up, giving in, or giving out.

These are leaders with grit and guts, having the tenacity and fortitude to pursue their goals regardless of the unknown. They don't buckle or fade, rust out or burn out, but they absorb the criticism, obstacles, setbacks, and funding challenges. They avoid interruptions and remove distractions; decisive and not hesitant, they constantly drive towards collecting wins, therefore increasing their team members' motivation. In the face of prevailing resource constraint, they cultivate a never-give-up mentality that allows them to create a mindset of abundance and a "let's do the thing" culture, motivating everyone to the winning path.

This mindset is built over time as they remain strategic, proactive, and focused on the finish line.

Because great leaders are focused, their time, energy, and activities are always aligned around the most critical priorities onsite. Through it all, they keep advancing, their eyes never leaving the goal while being open and willing to find creative solutions when things don't go as planned.

Here are the skills of relentless leaders that are integral to the successful execution of projects:

Relentless Leaders Have a Vision

When they visualize a project's result, they become relentless to see that what was visualized is made possible in reality. At every stage of the project, these leaders enact steps to successfully execute these projects because they already have a clear vision of the final result.

They Are a Bunch of Creatives

In the face of difficulties during project execution, they are relentless in coming up with innovative solutions to age-old problems rather than bang their heads against the wall while repeatedly trying the exact ineffective solutions. They keep pushing and trying out creative solutions to building infrastructures to meet their project goals even when the odds are against them.

They Are Focused

Irrespective of the dozens of workers they oversee, the tasks on schedule, numerous deadlines, and distractions fighting for their attention, they focus on meeting targets and reaching the overall goals. They are always careful to pick from dozens of ideas; they don't always say yes to the things they've got to focus on, but they weren't afraid of saying no to the hundred other good ideas that there are.

They Are Full of Courage

As stated previously, these leaders won't be relentless if they have no courage to take calculated risks, make smart moves, and approach difficult decisions and challenges with determination and confidence. Despite the obstacles in the way, their tenacious nature and daring act of defiance sets the ball rolling for their team, inspiring them towards productivity.

They Are Patient

Patience helps these leaders remain calm and sensible at critical moments on the job site. They embrace the power of patience because it eliminates the risk of making hasty decisions and errors. Thus, when they utilize their patience in such situations, they instantly gain and retain their team's respect while maintaining control of the project and tasks at hand.

They Can Be Relied Upon

Persistence is the ability to remain consistent even when confronted by multiple problems and complications, which establishes expectations from team members' actions.

Once you act and react to certain situations in a relatively similar perspective, you'll be perceived as being stable by subordinates; hence your stability can be relied upon.

Also, this persistence can become the team's tone of work. Through your actions and making specific choices that they expect, you establish a "can do" attitude. Once established, this tone becomes the expectation and operating principle for the team. They become unwilling to accept solutions beyond their ability. It also fuels their drive to seek solutions to problems that may arise in your absence and make them believe that project success is always possible.

7 | UPPER-LEVEL MINDSET

"These leaders have the mindset of moving on and reaching great altitudes, leaving behind the past."

For centuries, eagles have been fascinating birds, inspiring everyone with their brilliant leadership characteristics. Apparently, among the world's most giant birds of prey, they are revered as living symbols of power, freedom, bravery, courage, honor, determination, among others.

Each time they come to mind, they are well-known for their enormous hunting wings used for soaring and rising as the storm rages, unlike other birds that hide from the storm. These fascinating characteristics inspired the seventh undeniable trait of outstanding leadership.

Successful leaders in the industry aren't scared of moving on. Just like eagles, they are willing to soar effortlessly on upper-level currents. When others take cover from challenges or hide away from change and innovation, these leaders seize and leverage on thermal opportunities for updraft and lift.

They are open-minded and flexible to change, and hence they do not hang around with the rigid or fearful that are unwilling to change with the trend of innovation and technological advancement.

Great leaders understand the company's effect, thus staying away from narrow-minded people or those likely to bring them down. They fly and are a good company... with other eagles.

They are **problem solvers** and, thus, do not hang around on the ground complaining. They pick up the challenge that comes with change and find resolutions. Just like the eagle thrives in raging storms, these leaders are tenacious and thrive on challenges. They are not afraid of challenges; instead, they take pleasure in them, using them profitably as instruments to propel both themselves and their team forward.

These leaders have the mindset of moving on and reaching great altitudes, leaving behind the past. They do not rely on their past successes; they keep looking for new challenges and frontiers to conquer because they understand that these things will only make team members stronger and better as they keep rising to greater heights. Just like eagles, these leaders expand their minds and focus on things that matter as they soar.

They are eagles and hence do not peck with chickens or mingle with pigeons, sparrows, ravens, and other small birds. These birds scavenge on the ground, grumbling and complaining all day long. As eagles, these leaders do not do all of that. Instead, they are constantly on the lookout for opportunities.

They remain focused through the storm, finding a guide through it and staying motivated.

They keep putting the time, energy, and resources towards developing themselves and others to increase productivity, and they do this with less noise. Irrespective of the number of times they fail, these leaders do not hang onto their failures; instead, they keep working, learning, and never losing focus on the bigger picture.

In trying to move forward, some leaders get stuck at a certain level of their leadership and never master the next level. It is because they haven't examined the limitations, in the form of fear, habits, etc., holding them back. Once reviewed, these leaders know when and what to leave behind; they can overcome everything holding them back, leaving it behind to take their skills to the next level.

To be successful, here are a few things you need to leave behind to gain the ability to move on and focus on things that matter:

Past Defeats

Everyone faces setbacks and failures at some point, and it isn't a bad thing. Therefore, you shouldn't stay stuck agonizing over them. Rather, you should learn from these mistakes and risk-taking experiences, gaining wisdom that will gear you to a better path forward.

Critics

If not correctly spoken, words can be hurtful and destructive to anyone's life, and leaders are no exception. Most of them bear scars of hurtful words in their minds. As leaders, all eyes are on us, and we more likely to be criticized than anyone. Rather than allowing those words to get to you, build a resistance that absorbs these words without letting them hurt or stop you from doing what you can do. Worse of all, we are our own worst critics and often listen to our inner "self-doubting negative voice." However, we should learn to silence not only the voices around us but the ones in our heads as well.

Opposition

The industry continues to evolve daily; innovation and tech resources are available, but some good old-fashioned individuals are more likely to stick with the traditional way of doing things rather than adapt to the new changes. As a result, you are more likely to face opposition from these individuals. Instead of letting them stop progress and innovation, great leaders have an effective way of defeating and overcoming those that attempt to refuse changes.

Resistance works in two ways: we can use it to strengthen or weaken our resolve, and the choice is yours. Regardless of the opposition, it makes you sharper in thoughts, more intentional in actions, and more deliberate in making decisions. Hence, it would help if you didn't allow others' rigidity to cause doubt in your vision of a better future.

Distractions

To achieve leadership success, you must always stay committed to completing the important task at hand. It includes staying focused, determined, and not easily distracted. You should prioritize your activities and eliminate all possible distractions to achieve what you've always had in mind.

Thoughts of Disbelief

All successful projects begin with a positive mindset and belief. Every effective leader in the industry visualizes and believes in any building project before executing it. In thinking, these leaders shed off limiting mindsets and disbelief that can blur out that which was envisioned at the beginning.

7 | UPPER-LEVEL MINDSET

To become an effective leader, get committed to mastering the art of leaving behind and moving on, just like the eagle, because no one experiences success that wouldn't leave some things behind to move ahead. Do not hinder your ability to move forward by hanging onto less important things!

8 | HUMILITY

"If you think your way is the only way you really will not be able to build a team and you will not be successful at making a cohesive delivery of what you're trying to accomplish."
- Yehudi "Gaf" Gaffen
Gafcon, Inc., Founder and CEO

When recruiting for a leadership role, humility isn't the first trait that resonates through our minds. What comes to our mind is the perception of power and charisma above the team we lead. Some people even believe humility and leadership can't work together at the same time. Well, it can, and it is a MUST in leading successfully.

Humility gets a bad perception because it is sometimes linked with frailty or insecurity, but psychologically, humility is the opposite. While insecurity is tied to fear and our weaknesses, humility is a sign of great inner strength and confidence. It is always associated with a cluster of highly positive qualities mentioned in this book, such as openness, strength, courage, and authenticity, among others.

There's nothing about humility that makes it incompatible with strength and courage. It doesn't mean that humble leaders do not struggle with insecurities, but they also recognize that humility is based on strength rather than weakness.

So, what makes humility such an undeniable trait in the construction industry?

Simple. Humble leaders know how to get the most from the people they work with. Unlike other leaders in the industry whose subordinates are at the receiving end of their abuse of power and ego, humble leaders tend to influence more people to work with them.

How? There are several ways through which they do this, and here they are:

They Adopt the Humble Mindset

They adopt the humble mindset of a servant leader. They understand that they are not the most competent person on the team on every subject, so they encourage their team to speak up. They shift attention away from themselves and focus on their team's contributions, creating an environment where inputs are harnessed from everyone, opinions are respected, and the best ideas win, irrespective of if it came from a top executive or a lower-level staff. They recognize their weaknesses; hence, they readily seek input and have the confidence to admit that they can benefit from their team members' expertise and thus, actively seek their ideas and unique contributions.

Many leaders fail to understand the concept of humility; they end up expressing the "because I'm the boss" authority in their actions and words. It creates walls, distorts the flow of interaction, and lowers trust. Despite any number of certifications or the number of years in a leadership role, leaders should know that contractors and other employees who do the actual work during construction often know better than you how to do a great job.

8 | HUMILITY

They Ask Their Team What They Need

Rather than telling their team members how to do their jobs better, they start by asking their team members how they can help them do their jobs better. In doing that, these leaders eventually increase the ownership, independence, and responsibility of team members, so they become encouraged to think for themselves and try out their ideas. Over time, their team members become inspired to be their best.

The industry needs individuals who will inspire trust, cooperation, and commitment. One way to accomplish this is to help people feel purposeful, motivated, and energized to bring their best selves to work. Thus, the need to gain and develop humility is critical to earning more respect, confidence, and loyalty.

These leaders are not scared to turn to their team members for help and insights on the project because they understand their limitations. They do not see their limits as a sign of frailty but as an opportunity to benefit from their team members' complementary skills and ideas.

They Admit Their Mistakes

When they make mistakes, they also admit to their mistakes. They know they are human, hence are prone to making mistakes from time to time. They are willing to own up to their mistakes, allowing their team to see their flawed humanity and recognizing there's always room for improvement. This action might make some feel vulnerable, but it connects them with their team in a more profound way.

Over time these leaders become self-aware. They know who they are, and they put efforts towards behaving in a way that's consistent with that knowledge in terms of respect, support and service. With such consistency, they begin gaining and earning trust from everyone around.

They Appreciate Team Members

A humble leader is able to create an aura of teamwork, where team members are appreciated and credit is given to those who deserve it. They are not always out to take credit but to give, which doesn't affect their position as a leader. As team members get credit for their ideas and see their ideas put into place, they become more impressed, respected, and willing to offer more ideas.

Who wouldn't want a healthy working environment, free from harsh words, fear, and egoistic leaders?

Leaders lacking in humility are not overly obsessed with outcomes and control and, as such, treat their team members harshly. When team members are fearful, it impacts their productivity as they stop feeling positive emotions, and their drive to experiment and learn is stifled. No matter how long you've been in your role, if this happens, you will become merely a figurehead unless you bring out the best in your team.

They Are Not Easily Embarrassed

Humble leaders are not easily embarrassed as they possess a healthy balance of self-awareness and self-confidence. They are not offended if they don't receive credit because they serve others' good rather than work for accolades. These leaders promote every member of their team and are not prone to put others down to gain an advantage or maneuver in position. Since humility comes from strength, these leaders have a good self-image of who they are, but they do not constantly tell others of their worth, accomplishments, or importance. They do not use their influence, authority, and power to gain or take advantage of their team members.

Humility doesn't call for flattery because these leaders know the importance of being genuine and authentic; there is a consistency of such traits, not just with their team or when on site. They are the same person, be it in private or public, with every person, and in all types of situations.

With humility, they increase collaboration, cooperation, and flexibility in developing and advancing a project's execution, both commercially and residentially.

Practical Steps

- When things go wrong, admit to your mistakes and take responsibility. When things go right, shine the spotlight on others. Avoid passing blame and exempting yourself from responsibility.

- Give credit by acknowledging the contributions of others in helping to achieve success.

- Accept and respond positively to constructive feedback by acknowledging the feedback's validity and demonstrating a thoughtful response.

- Avoid putting down others through gossip or different ways.

- Once weaknesses are pointed out, overcome them by trying to improve.

No doubt we are impressed by charismatic candidates with influential personalities and a commanding presence. However, to streamline processes and ensure timely delivery, you need to be humble enough to listen more effectively, respect team members' ideas, and inspire great teamwork. These efforts will ensure project progress and improvement while encouraging team members to be innovative and try new things.

That's where outstanding leadership begins.

9 | PATIENCE

"Influential leaders do not allow such pressures to push them to make hasty decisions because they understand impatience's consequences."

We often talk about patience like it is an easy thing to do, but we find it challenging to practice it, especially during difficult situations. It is due to how we live in a society where actions and decisions are taken quickly; everyone wants immediate results. It builds pressure, and leaders are no exception to these expectations.

Every leader in the industry feels the pressure of building the most effective teams, creating a high-performance environment, and efficiently utilizing available site resources to execute projects successfully.

This pressure often causes emotions to rise as tempers flare and harsh words are used, especially when work becomes tough. The root of this crisis and problem is impatience. Leaders in the industry who cannot practice patience will find their careers short-lived. The industry demands it because patience is required to create long-term value. Team members also need leaders to have it, or they won't see you as a compassionate leader who is open-minded and can manage any circumstance.

Patience is a virtue and a leader who practices it has the pearl of wisdom like a bone in his throat. Being capable of enduring difficulty and hardship while calmly awaiting the appropriate opportunity to act is a trait found lacking among leaders in the industry today. Patience is one of the many characteristics that contribute immensely to many great leadership successes in the industry.

Influential leaders do not allow such pressures to push them to make hasty decisions because they understand the consequences of impatience. Undoubtedly, people will criticize and condemn their perceived inaction or lack of speed. Still, with composure and character, these leaders wait, take stock of the scenario, and understand what is required before taking appropriate and effective action.

From strategic planning to team development, negotiations, and program management, all tasks associated with a project's execution require patience. Patience is needed to remain committed to the end, irrespective of the time and planning duration of the issues that might affect the project.

By demonstrating patience, these leaders emphasize the importance of focusing on long-term outcomes. Hence, they understand that patience may require sacrificing short-term glory to reach such long-term results. After visualizing the desired end-state of a project, they do not jump ahead without exercising the patience needed. To actualize the work, they have built their minds to work and wait. Otherwise, they become impatient and fail in their endeavors.

Though patience is focused on the result, it doesn't mean ignoring the interim milestones or short-term deliverables; it means keeping them in context. Apart from the results, having excellent skills in patience will create the best kind of team. Having the patience to listen to your team members communicate shows respect and that you value their opinions. Tolerance also increases productivity. Team members will not strive in a work environment of frustration, rush, or fear; you can obtain the best results with patience and deliberate instructions.

Patience also inspires them to positivity, especially during difficult times. If your team notices your calm and patient demeanor during adversity, they remain optimistic, patient, and confident too. If you can't retain your composure in the face of frustration, you won't be able to keep them calm.

Leading effectively takes patience, and these leaders often practice it in several ways:

They See Through the Lens of Others

Whenever certain circumstances occur, rather than judge and share their opinions about how they should manage, great leaders become objective enough to step back, remove themselves from their personal views, and then begin to see the situation through the lenses of other people.

And even if they lose their cool or grow impatient, these leaders must handle the pressure, be wise to be accountable, and resolve the issue immediately.

They Evaluate and Connect the Dots Toward an Eventual Solution in an Unbiased Way

These leaders practice patience by remaining unbiased while carefully evaluating tension points in any given crisis. They don't choose sides. Instead, they are extremely open-minded and always mindful of their team's specific needs, approach, and style. Also, because they are patient under pressure, they are often able to see previously unseen opportunities in the midst of problems. They see the bigger picture, help, and appreciate their team. It builds self-trust overtime.

They Listen and Ask Questions

Practicing patience, these leaders are required to be great listeners. Despite the room's tension and pressure, they take a deep breath and let go of their impatience to solve a problem. They aren't in a hurry, and they ask lots of questions to ensure issues are resolved properly.

These Leaders Are Positive

Negativity, showing frustration, or playing victims aren't plays in their books. They show up with a positive attitude by being hospitable and expressing it with a smile. It has a fantastic effect on the practice of patience, and it blossoms relationships and encourages productivity.

They Don't Pretend to Know All the Answers

In severe scenarios, they do not force their authority on others to push the problem away; they seek further advice from a trusted resource, maybe a mentor, who can add value and provide them with needed perspective. They see these challenging moments as opportunities to learn about themselves and others, develop patience, and gain perspective.

They Are Accountable

As leaders, they have the power to take direction well or always make excuses, yet they do not take advantage of such power by running away from being responsible themselves if it's their fault. When you practice patience in such a situation, it becomes a journey of understanding where everyone collaboratively solves problems, which will earn you respect from everyone.

Practical Steps

Understand the situation and establish the facts: your ability to lead patiently requires the skill to manage whatever situation you may find yourself in. You can't manage a situation if you do not understand it. Leverage your skills and your team members' skills to have an in-depth understanding of any case, the importance of the problem that might arise, and how urgent the resolution is needed.

Create a plan and execute it: knowing where you are going also requires patience and drawing up a project plan. After you have created it, have the confidence to stick to it and deliver; when adversity arises, hold your ground.

10 | VISION

"A shared vision gives a clear purpose to a group on what to do. It also unites them and enables them by giving them glimpses of "what is possible."

Leadership in the industry is about innovating, creating, building, improving, and transforming structures whether it is commercial or residential. It begins with visualizing. It includes imagination, big but seemingly impossible ideas, and dreams woven together to build jaw-dropping structures.

Industry leaders tap into the power of vision to find a way forward through the hurdles. It enables them to harness the power of positivity as they lead, inspiring and transforming their teams while achieving significant results.

These leaders see what is possible and then take the next steps to rally and unite their team to create it.

They understand that project creation or transformation starts with imagination, an idea, and a vision of what's possible. In having a mental picture of the result, you also have the power to make it happen; hence they articulately communicate that picture in a transparent, bold, and compelling way to their team, so they all work together in actualizing it. Everyone associated with the project can be more effective if they understand a set of shared goals and actualize it. Those goals require planning, which includes not only "why" we are doing this, but also "where" we are all going. Vision is what leaders use to develop a plan to communicate to the rest of the team so everyone knows where they're headed. Having your team's input is highly valuable and necessary, but your vision as the leader ensures progress and improvement on the job daily.

Without vision, there is no room for improvement. You can't hit something you don't aim for. Based on industry culture and the current state of world economies, visions can also ensure that any project's goals are realistic.

Vision drives everything. It embodies hopes and ideas, and a leader with a vision can achieve more significant results with efforts from the team they lead. A shared vision gives a clear purpose to a group on what to do. It also unites them and enables them by giving them glimpses of "what is possible," inspiring the power and energy to get the work done.

Vision fuels the drive, and without it, everyone becomes unmotivated and uninspired. To get motivated and always inspired to keep going, these leaders keep the result in their minds, and this is what gets them up in the morning and carries them through to the end. And with such a vibe, there isn't going to be any slacking from the team members.

Your vision will stretch your team's abilities, challenging them to try new things and allowing them to grow themselves, and when you throw in a good goal together with the idea, you will build a team that is excited to come to work every day.

Apart from seeing the big picture and all the parts that make up the big picture, these leaders also see the strengths and weaknesses of individuals and the team in general, thereby understanding how things work or don't work so they can make big decisions to address them and improve upon them as they move forward.

These leaders can see beyond what's possible today and look toward what is possible in the future. They can also see the path that their team must be on to get there; this is because vision gives direction. It shows where you are all headed so everyone can look forward to it. With such an approach, everyone stays on course and is also enabled and prepared for rocky times or unexpected setbacks. With a strong vision, obstacles and setbacks become a learning opportunity as everyone would learn from it as they work and persevere through such hurdles.

Create a vision and read it countless times until it gets stuck in your head. Pasting it on a wall or placing it in a team member's welcome packet is not enough. It would help if you made your team buy into the idea, drilling this vision into them so they believe it, and often checking to make sure it's being understood and is effective. If not, they'll pack up and leave.

Having a firm conviction towards a goal provides you with an intense focus and a sense of accomplishment. Once you begin acting on this vision, you become focused, vying away from distractions that steal our attention in our world today. You get to thrash out or delegate mundane stuff and give full attention to what is essential to achieve the results.

Often, most inexperienced leaders fail to communicate their vision appropriately to their team. As a result, they end up with a confused team or a team where everyone starts to create their own direction. When everyone is pulled in many different directions, some of these directions will cancel each other out, and thus, even if much work is being done, very little is being accomplished. This problem might mainly be due to not having a vision themselves rather than a lack of communication.

It is much easier to lead if you have a clear idea of what you want to achieve and then conveying such to the people you lead. No one wants to follow a person without a plan. By having a clear vision of what you want to accomplish, irrespective of if you don't have a tremendous amount of skill as a leader, you'll attract others because people often align themselves with someone who articulates a vision.

Who wouldn't want to join in success? People want to follow someone who will lead them to win, and if you are perceived to be able to do this, people will like to follow you. A new leader with a great vision tends to be more successful than an established leader with a vague plan. When it comes to having a track record of success, your many mistakes or poor leadership habits can be forgotten as everyone will stick with you to succeed.

Many people often mistake success for good leadership skills. Unfortunately, people want to follow people who can be successful even if they have lousy leadership skills. They may sometimes start mimicking some of your poor leadership habits, thinking they are part of the reason for your success.

Please understand me. Good leadership skills are critical, but your skills might be useless without a clear vision because it won't be worth it for your team to work with you.

Practical Steps

A practical exercise that you can use to develop and hone your creative communication skills:

Step 1: Think of a challenge associated with the project at hand.

Step 2: Imagine the big picture. No dream is too big or too fantastic. Visualize the incredible future success of such a project.

Step 3: Determine and write out how you will communicate your vision to your team. Carefully choose the words, phrases, and the environment to share your vision.

Step 4: Practice communicating what you have written. Be sure it sounds sincere. You could also practice with others and get feedback from them. Communicating frequently will enable you to express your vision in a compelling but precise manner.

Step 5: Communicate your vision; let it inspire, not dictate. Give the gift and benefits of the invention, not the actions. Let them figure that out.

11 | IN ACTION

"Actions speak louder than words. Your team members will listen to what you say, but they will pay more attention to what you do."

Leadership is both rewarding and challenging. Since the industry is result-oriented, taking immediate action and executing projects is critical. Hence, being a leader emphasizes a step toward more responsibility, and it provides greater visibility for your getting things done and your style of making a difference.

Successful leaders within the industry effectively establish their style, values, and culture quickly so that everyone in the team does what they need to stay on track and meet deadlines.

They don't sit and watch; they act! Actions speak louder than words. Your team members will listen to what you say, but they will pay more attention to what you do.

With such an understanding, these leaders put in the work and attention to hitting deadlines and executing projects after making sound decisions during the project planning. Not only do they get things done without losing focus or getting lost in the weeds of distractions, they engage and energize everyone while providing visible evidence of a strong, action-oriented culture.

One way to effectively establish your desired work culture is through action. To improve on execution and become more execution-focused to take immediate action, these leaders focus on the following:

Delegate and Empower Others When Possible

Although leaders do not necessarily make all the decisions, their job is to ensure decisions happen. It is even preferable if leaders do **not** make most of the findings but get others to be empowered so delegation can occur. First, they establish an exact measurement criterion, then provide them with information, resources, and the necessary level of trust to make decisions in their spheres of influence.

It empowers the team to act and be more creative, dynamic, and solution-oriented since they don't need to wait for the leader's approval to execute when they're ready. At the same time, the leader holds them accountable to that criterion based on their roles and responsibilities. Within this culture, everyone learns and becomes more engaged as everyone begins to decide on solutions rather than simply identify problems and have endless discussions.

Since formulating actions comes with accountability, if there is no clear accountability, decisions and actions will often fail.

Take Immediate Action

No matter of how little tasks are, these leaders do not underestimate the effect of acting on small things. After discussions are made and everyone has agreed on what needs to be done, they work immediately by doing it or delegating it.

Set Priorities

On the table of a leader is a huge workload, but these leaders, having the mindset of taking immediate action, won't start too many tasks simultaneously. Instead, they articulate the larger priorities by delegating small things to free them from focusing on more extensive issues.

Define Alternatives

Often it can be challenging to make decisions during a discussion. Sometimes, your team cannot take immediate action.

In this case, leaders start the decision process by ensuring everyone agrees to the alternatives provided. Then they determine additional information needed to select a solution and the individual responsible for following through. Then they schedule a date to continue to review the additional information and then make a final decision before execution begins.

They Remain Influenceable

These leaders understand they aren't superhuman with super cognitive powers. They can't know everything. This knowledge enables them to try out several options in the form of suggested inputs and information from others, all of which will modify their direction and decision. As stated earlier, such actions will also increase trust as they will establish a decision culture, improve teamwork, and empower everyone while increasing engagement for project execution.

Practical Steps

Fine-tune your communication with the team to better delegate, execute, and act.

To bring execution to the forefront, you first have to communicate, starting with goal-setting and aligning priorities and resources. Bring on the team and all other stakeholders directly involved in the project board. This communication should be immediate and consistent. You could use available tools that can keep communication at your fingertip. You need to stay connected with all parties because to be execution-focused, you need to move fast. When formulating an action to delegate, name just one person to start that action, otherwise the action might not have an accountable party when reporting results. While naming one person to start, also name out those who'd assist in order to reinforce teamwork.

Set a Date

When delegating actions, do not leave such tasks open-ended; always ask for a target date when you will take the next step. Without a set target date of completion, there would be very little action taken.

Establish Checkpoints for Review Processes

Create a measurement criterion like a checkpoint where you will review progress and issues; this will not only keep the activity moving but enable mid-course corrections and resolve issues.

Set One-On-One Feedback Meetings

It could be monthly or quarterly, but make these meetings a two-way conversation where you allow team members to improve, along with yourself. This will enable you to build a work culture where everyone gets better after knowing what isn't working.

Take Corrective Measures

One way to improve accountability and energize everyone to act is to deal with poor performers. It would be best if you started with individuals that almost everyone can identify are not meeting expectations on projects before setting the process to take corrective action of coaching and training.

Apart from knowing lackadaisical individuals that others know well, you can also review their performance appraisal process and assure that it is rigorous and timely.

The Delegated Task Should Remain Delegated

While you handle your tasks as leaders, tasks you have delegated shouldn't have to be done by you irrespective of the submission mistakes and errors. When the person accountable did not do an adequate job, provide them with additional information, context, or help and send them back to try again rather than doing the job yourself. While you act based on your role, empower your team to do the same rather than avoid it.

12 | DECISIVE

"These leaders have diligently worked on certain crucial qualities that developed them to become great decision-makers."

A vital aspect of being successful in the industry as a leader is a decisive attribute. Decisiveness is key for effectively executing plans, achieving project goals, and leading a company.

We do not envision leaders just standing still and ordering everyone around while appearing unclear and uncertain. Instead, we view leaders as individuals who can make time-sensitive and well-informed decisions and communicate the goals to others. Thus, decisiveness is one of those traits that are extremely important to great leadership in the industry, and a lack of it can be devastating and frustrating, which is detrimental to the business.

To be decisive, leaders seek out the appropriate information that is necessary to make a good decision and also balance out emotion with reason to make that decision to positively impact not only the project but themselves, their team, and every other stakeholder involved.

Their approach towards decision-making involves an understanding that their team needs to be valued, respected, listened to, and interested in being able to make sound decisions themselves, which results in a more streamlined outcome.

Making good decisions, especially in difficult situations, can be challenging because these decisions involve uncertainty, change, anxiety, stress, and sometimes adverse reactions from others. Leaders are aware of the costs of each decision they make. Hence, they weigh them carefully, and sometimes, deliberately delay a decision to avoid making poor choices.

Leaders know when to make decisions quickly with the available information and when to pause in order to take more time to gather more information. In gathering more information, they also know when to stop in order not to waste too much time that can shift their focus away from the big picture.

As humans, we have an inherent fear of making mistakes, and that is the most common reason why some leaders are unable to move forward with decisions or prolong the decision-making process. However, these leaders have diligently worked on certain crucial qualities that developed them to become great decision-makers.

Emotional Intelligence

One essential skill these leaders possess to become decisive is understanding, managing, and controlling their emotions to adapt to change and adopt an optimistic outlook. Emotions are known to cloud our ability to make decisions. Still, in developing this skill of emotional self-control, you'll be able to recognize your feelings instead of becoming too blinded by emotion. For instance, when presented with a critical challenge onsite, which tends to be a significant potential downside, of course, this causes a rush of adrenaline that makes us more likely to feel angry, anxious, or afraid. Being in this state is not particularly conducive to making strategic, long-term decisions because we might become blinded by it.

But honing this skill will enable us to be aware of our emotional state and manage intense emotions to calmly and clearly express smart decisions.

It doesn't mean you shouldn't experience emotion in such a situation or take the feelings out of the decision-making process; that would backfire and make you feel worse. Instead, it means sorting it out head-on but keeping these emotions from taking over and making you lose control. Once ridden out, the intensity of these emotions will quickly pass, and then you can think logically. It all begins with knowing how to bring down intense emotions so that you can look at the big picture and focus on facts before plunging head-long into a decision.

The Ability to Handle Uncertainty and Change

Decision-making becomes difficult for most people because its variables and outcomes are uncertain and liable to change, creating discomfort. Sometimes, leaders bury their heads in the sand and believe a decision for a change or new direction isn't necessary, hence avoid it or stick with the "usual." Uncertainties especially paralyze us and make us base our decisions on things that aren't even related to seeking a false sense of security.

To handle uncertainty, these leaders accept it rather than try to resolve it and focus their time, energy, and money on making the best decisions in the face of an uncertain outcome.

This does not imply that they don't analyze a situation before deciding. Leaders certain analyze the situation, especially if what they don't know is important. Analyzing the situation helps provide them with the necessary information needed to make the best decisions in any given case. However, if what they don't know is unimportant, they accept the uncertainty and move on despite it.

One of the decision-making mistakes we commonly make is considering every possible alternative, giving ourselves many options. We assume that we will be left with better choices if we go through everything and make the best decision. This is overwhelming, and often, we end up not making any decision. Thus, you need to limit your options, preferably keeping them fewer than five, so it won't be as challenging to decide.

The Ability to Weigh Evidence with Intuition

No one likes to work with leaders who can't make up their minds or leaders who always ask everyone what they thought about something but never reach any conclusions themselves. Great leaders have, over time, built themselves to trust their guts to make excellent decisions. Their guts are mainly dependent on their expertise. The more they know, the more reliable their intuition will be, feeling a lot happier and relieved rather than being stuck with over-thinking.

In our busy and non-stop technologically filled industry, hearing your intuition can turn out more demanding because the gut feeling speaks softly within us, which we may not take notice of due to external interference. These decisive leaders immensely use their guts feeling as a guide because they often hone their skill of listening to it. They do this by imbibing moments of reflection and other meditative practices into their daily lives to feel themselves into hearing themselves. Leaders know when to press pause, quiet the noise, and lean in to make a decision.

Being decisive takes much practice, and its process requires a certain level of comfort with discomfort. So rather than spending time and effort playing it safe by analyzing every option, you can accept the risks involved and go for it. Even if you make a terrible decision or take a wrong move, it should be a learning opportunity for you. You can also find unexpected opportunities by going down the "wrong" path. So decide your way to great decisions and be a great leader by committing to make difficult decisions promptly.

13 | FUN

"Fun is a factor in productive living; it makes team members more energized and focused and more willing and able to get more done."

Fun! The word alone makes one giggle as everyone has some attachment to it. Each of us, no doubt, carries fond memories of fun moments and fun times with fun people. When such memories are repeated at work, no one would love only to rush home.

When working, our moods change and sometimes morph in reaction to a circumstance or action from the people around us. Having fun activities occasionally mixed with work makes everything more enjoyable. Fun is a factor in productive living; it makes team members more energized and focused and more willing and able to get more done.

If properly utilized, the fun can be a very effective tool in a leader's toolbox to lead to greater productivity by happier people. So, great leaders learn how to utilize fun as a tool to enrich and entertain team members. It's fun to have fun, and these leaders know it can't be fun when something important is amiss. For instance, team members cannot sincerely laugh while worrying, hurting, or regretting. That's not called fun. If the condition and atmosphere aren't suitable, then fun won't make much of a difference in their lives.

Great leaders have a means of arranging circumstances that are likely to produce fun, which lifts any form of heaviness that can cause tardiness, negativity, or toxic attitude. However, work and fun do not have to be two different activities. If we are having fun while working, the energy and motivation to get the job done becomes higher, and more is done. Leaders who understand this inject it into work situations at just the right time to diffuse tense moments and make work more attractive.

Also, effective leaders know that their team members would rarely succeed if what they are doing isn't fun to them. Who would stay in a job that brings no joy? No one! Such a person is more likely looking for something else.

When we do what we are built to do or called to do, we will be deeply motivated to do it and hence, enjoy it. These leaders understand that working in the area of one's natural gifts is often the most fun, so they will ensure their team members are correctly arranged in their positions based on their skills and talents. Although this takes much work, they put effort into making it work so the concept of fun can dominate their thoughts and speeches.

They also understand how to have fun and induce fun in the lives of their team members. They know when to lighten the mood and make the shared tasks of their teams enjoyable. As a result, these leaders rouse a sense of belonging among team members, ensure better mental health for them, and relieve any form of tension that prohibits productive action and creative thinking.

13 | FUN

When team members have a good time at work, they are more engaged, refreshed, and rejuvenated and become more productive. Having fun also reduces stress that impairs decision-making and causes poorer communication, more job accidents, increased time off, and other health problems.

These benefits leave leaders responsible for creating, inserting, and increasing opportunities for fun and enjoyment. Team members have to increase team engagement and productivity.

Here are ways these leaders interject doses of fun in the industry corporate culture:

They Look for Fun

These leaders pay attention to their team members' attitudes, watch their working style, and notice the enjoyment and fun they derive from it. Also, they help their team members recognize the joy in what they do!

They Promote Fun

When these leaders see any joy in at least some of their work, they promote it by letting everyone know it is a good thing and giving them the space to play a bit. It allows them to continue to inject some playful and fun banter or conversation into work rather than expecting them to be all serious-minded. This act automatically creates an environment of both fun and effectiveness, where everyone is energized and motivated to get started and work every day. Some leaders assume that a relaxed work environment automatically implies everyone will be lackadaisical towards work, and hence there will be a lack of productivity, but that is false! A relaxed work environment is a breath of fresh air from the stiffness that might cause anxiety, worry, or mistakes. The lighter the work environment, the better your team will perform.

They Model Fun

Leaders are meant to lead the way in all things, and fun isn't excluded. To enable team members to have fun, these leaders generate and model the energy and enthusiasm that is key to creating a fun environment that everyone would love to work in. They are pretty aware that their team members look to them for cues on how to act and thus, pick up their vibe, disposition, and demeanor. Therefore, if they are not having fun, their team members will not too; you can't model something else.

To model fun, you have to enjoy what you do. Have a great time on the job so that it doesn't feel like work. Like you can't believe that you are getting paid to do what you love to do. This vibe will spread to your team members, and they would adopt this same mentality and perspective.

They Create Fun

Regardless of how team members derive fun during work time, these leaders also look for ways to put more fun into the work. It could be a surprise outing or something viewed as fun by others. To effectively select an event that everyone loves and sees as fun, these leaders organize a fun committee where volunteers create occasional and appropriate activities to inject enjoyment and fun into the work.

We, as leaders, are tasked with the responsibility of building fun environments that will inspire, encourage, and motivate team members to be creative and give their best effort daily. As a way of having fun, we also have to enthusiastically embrace the great things that come our way onsite or offsite. We have a specific intent or desire in meeting all challenges with a positive mental attitude, and this spreads out to those we work with. As a result, every minute becomes valuable, productive, and worthwhile.

Practical Steps

Here are just a few of the many ways you can incorporate fun and camaraderie into the workplace. Not only will these help to lighten the mood, but they will help team members become more connected and promote a positive work culture where we work hard and play hard!

- Office Chair relay race
- Egg drops
- Lip sync battles
- Board games
- Pub Thursdays
- Workplace decoration: creative cubicles, fresh flowers, etc.
- Employee "Wall of Fame"
- Humor bulletin board, started fresh each week
- Trivia nights
- Finding opportunities that will help personal development
- Milestone celebrations with pizza parties, ice cream, etc.
- Outdoor sports tournaments and matches
- Birthday festivities and acknowledgment
- Page per day calendars
- Award ceremonies
- Annual team vacations or outings

14 | EFFECTIVELY COMMUNICATE

"Do you know that 98% of what we communicate is non-verbal? Communication isn't all about spoken or written words."

It is simply impossible to become a great leader without being a great communicator! Communication is vital for leaders to excel. Often, we think we're good and excelling in this trait, but in reality, we aren't. It takes practice and a conscious effort to be a great communicator.

Being a great communicator doesn't mean being a great talker; instead, it is a two-way thing. We've been constantly taught, from pre-kindergarten, that communication is all about us, our opinions, positions, and circumstances. So, all we do is talk, talk, and talk! However, communication in leadership doesn't focus on ourselves but others.

The message being passed is not about us as leaders; it has nothing to do with us. It is more about paying keen interest to others, understanding their concerns, and asking questions before using our skills and expertise to craft an intentional response that will add value to their world. By doing this, team members become encouraged and stimulated to act responsibly. Tasks become less burdensome, and everyone checks in with each other to ensure that the job is moving forward smoothly.

Effective communication is so important that it determines professional success, including a broader circle of our team members' influence. Most successful leaders spend 80% of their time in meetings and interacting with their teams, individually or in-group. It shows the importance of communicating effectively; that's the bulk of the job! These leaders are quite aware of this, and that's why they spend time and effort developing themselves to be great communicators. With effective communication skills, it becomes much easier to work toward the best outcome with team members.

Leaders with great communication skills might talk about their ideas, aspirational vision, or a well-thought-out strategy. Still, they also keep relationship management in mind, and thus, speak to their team's emotions and aspirations. They do not muddle through their interactions with others. Rather, they possess a heightened sense of situational awareness.

No matter how comprehensive and detailed your strategy is, it won't translate to reality if you cannot communicate the strategy effectively. Inability to communicate effectively can hinder a leader's performance more than anything. In times of crisis where they are responsible for handling every situation, they get critical information across quickly with concise and clear communication that is spoken calmly.

In becoming great communicators, these leaders have the habit of:

Listening Intently

Listening is the number one habit of all great communicators; it separates one as a good communicator and a good talker. By listening intently to things most people ignore, they get vital messages that are more likely to be missed when only "hearing." As they listen, they become focused and intentional with their words and actions, eliminating any form of assumptions. They also understand more about each team member's personality types and then utilize communication styles that suit individual members, thereby enabling perfect and precise communication.

Paying Attention to Body Language

Do you know that 98% of what we communicate is non-verbal? Communication isn't all about spoken or written words; body language is the most important factor in communicating. Effective leaders know this. Therefore, they pay keen attention to their team members' body language because it sheds light on what they are thinking and feeling at that point. Also, they pay attention to their body language because they understand that their team member is more likely to be interested in what they say if these leaders give out a positive and powerful body language.

Using the "You" and "We" Word

These leaders understand the message is not focused on them but has more to do with the audience. Thus, they use words like "you" and "we" word more than "I" and "me."

Looking Out for Key Takeaways

Effective communication is the heart of successful leadership within the industry, and these leaders make it a habit to pass clear, concise, and conclusive messages to team members. They do not struggle with the proper amount of communication; instead, they ensure they deliver vital messages to team members.

Often Repeating Standards and Expectations

These leaders often communicate their expectations to their team; they don't expect them to know what they are thinking. Once they set and maintain high standards for themselves and their team members, they also communicate with them repeatedly, all the time, until it feels like a broken record to the ears of everyone.

Seeking and Telling Stories

A great way to communicate effectively is via stories because it speaks to our emotions. It inspires and makes one think and feel. Stories enable leaders to express their plans in a way that will stick in the minds of team members, helping them remember ideas and concepts easily.

Being Open and Upfront with Team Members

Transparency in leadership sparks impressive results that benefit everyone involved in a project. Great leaders understand that, so they are willing to be honest and open with their team, even if it feels somewhat vulnerable. They strive to practice what they preach, set clear expectations, and communicate effectively with every member of their team. As a result, there are no unpleasant surprises, misunderstandings, unmet expectations, or concerns around uncertainty. In this setting, team members get to be in the loop, and they are updated on the good and bad. As a result, team members feel valued and open to giving honest feedback. It fosters a work culture of accountability and open communication for everyone as team members give their loyalty and trust.

Irrespective of your role or position within the industry, you are more than just a boss! You communicate as you move through each stage of executing projects, directing your team to work together to meet targets and deadlines. You being a floppy communicator will affect everything, so invest in becoming a great communicator. It is worth your constant effort and attention, so you'll become better equipped to guide your team in the right direction and execute your team's strategy.

Practical Steps

Communication skills are one of the skills that most leaders have the most significant weakness in. You may ask, *"How do I know when my skills have matured to the extent of becoming an excellent communicator?"*

Here are a few ways you can improve your communication skill:

- Get personal and specific. Take time to know team members personally, meet with them one-on-one, and establish a personal connection.

- Have an open mind but read between the lines. Identify body language cues.

- Be quiet and listen attentively.

- Replace ego with empathy.

- When you speak, know what you're talking about. Don't speak with a forked tongue.

- Change the message if needed but be intentionally creative, engaging, and fun.

- Speak to groups as individuals and be attentive to what inspires them.

- Model the behaviors that you want to promote by talking about the "why" as often as possible so that team members can tie your words to the main task.

- Ask questions, even when you think that you know the answer. Also, lead people to the answer to figure it out themselves instead of just telling them.

15 | EMPOWER

"Let's look at it strategically at how moving forward we can be successful and how I can help you be successful."
- Marty Glaske, Senior Vice President,
Client Development of Gafcon, Inc.

We live in a modern-day society filled with competition, self-centeredness, and self-obsession. Many people do not hesitate to tear down or destroy others to be successful within the industry. From spreading negative stories, passing blame, or becoming toxic or a critic to ideas, all of which are inclined to pull others down, they remain unscathed. However, leaders who are defying this notion, becoming people-oriented by mastering the ability to lift and build others up, are the ones who turn out to be effective and successful. This trait is undeniably one of the qualities that form the basis for a productive team, successful projects, and a successful company.

Empowering leaders realize the team doesn't exist to make them celebrities. The job isn't all about them; it is about their team members. So rather than using their position of power for personal gain, they serve, and in helping their team members, they understand part of their job is to inspire and motivate them. These are leaders who seek to find and highlight their team members' good and positive attributes and support their development to become better at who they are (as humans) and what they do onsite.

These leaders are impactful, taking their team to heights they would not reach individually on their own or as a team. With proper guidance, the team doesn't simply become more productive, they enjoy every step of the project execution process.

Creating the Right Work Environment

Empowering leaders begin lifting their team members by putting efforts into creating environments where the best attributes of these individuals, no matter how small, are placed on luminous display for all—an environment that encourages openness and teamwork, free of any toxicity. Toxic attitudes like gossip or rumors can cause unnecessary hurt to others and pull anyone down.

Believe in Your Team Members

As good leaders, they often see where people can best use their gifts, and they help team members get to those spots. They need a team to succeed, and the team needs confidence to grow. These leaders are aware that a strong belief in their team members' capacities goes a long way to boost their morale and skyrocket productivity. Since you believe in them, they'll naturally want to justify that belief. Hence, they'll work a little harder, try one more time, and give a little extra overall. So, if you genuinely believe in them, share such belief with them, and then watch as they soar.

Reward and Celebrate Strengths and Successes

These leaders also lift others by becoming a cheerleader for their team members, highlighting their good and positive attributes, celebrating every big or small "score" they achieve. This act doesn't threaten these leaders; they do not hoard the spotlight or seek credit for themselves. Instead, they give praise for work well done, celebrate individual strengths, and look for ways to allow every team member to shine with their unique skill sets.

This type of approach creates an atmosphere where everyone is appreciated. These attitudes also birth the creation of leaders beneath them, not followers. Some leaders would feel insecure or threatened, and thus, they suppress others and would rather keep team members in check rather than allow them to have growth opportunities. Influential leaders know that this is a win-win for everyone, such that we also rise as we lift them. When you allow team members to reach their full potential, we are more likely to make more leaders within our ranks.

Be Their Co-pilot

Leaders who lift their team members happen to journey with them through to the end of the project. They support them during adversity, console them at each defeat, and are a rock to them during an emotional rollercoaster. They are consistent in being there for their team members even if, of course, it is not always physically. Check-ins, in the form of a call, though not before a big deadline or during a scheduled conference call, are advisable. These leaders aren't too busy to forget, and if they are, they put a reminder in their calendar a few times a month.

Stretch Them to Do a Little More

Another way these leaders lift their team members is by driving them past their comfort zone into new opportunity for achievement. They train, coach, and mentor their team and demonstrate how to navigate uncertain terrains and new processes that can make one struggle. They start by establishing a sincere rapport over time before they set a goal. Once the plan has been established, they ask for the team members' permission to hold them accountable and push them to achieve the goal. To challenge them doesn't mean you have to discourage them; it means you genuinely care about them and are willing to fuel their drive to conquer new grounds.

Share Knowledge

Another way these influential leaders lift others is by freely sharing their knowledge and experience with them. Rather than hoarding knowledge and information to prevent their subordinates from advancing, these leaders openly share insights, knowledge, and experiences with their team members for the benefit of all. It enhances team members' proactiveness and enables them to solve problems in the leader's absence and create better results overall. Sharing knowledge could be a presentation about a seminar/workshop lecture, an article, or a book you find helpful. With access to the internet, sharing has been made easier via web tools and social media sites.

Delegate

Good leaders aren't afraid to admit they are humans and don't know everything nor can they do it all alone. They are willing to learn from someone when they are better at a project, have a more creative approach, or are more experienced with a task. Because they don't know everything, they listen and do not dismiss their team's opinions and feedback, irrespective of the level or position, and then delegate tasks appropriately.

Just as Jim Stovall once stated, "In being aware of what your team members are doing, you should encourage them in their pursuits, applaud their efforts, and acknowledge their successes; and with that, everyone wins!"

Practical Steps

- Practice going around, onsite or offsite, and say, "I believe in you," or "you can do this."

- Build positivity through words and action.

- Communicate effectively.

- Watch your comments by thinking before you speak.

- Start with praise.

- Never confront; instead, point out how you and they can make things better.

- Do not come in with an authoritative voice to get your message heard.

- Listen.

- Do not plan a reply as one is speaking.

- Ask intelligent questions to gain further insight.

- Hold your team members in high esteem.

- Have high regards, great respect, and good thoughts of team members.

- Have weekly information and knowledge sharing.

- Going one step further, visualize how you can build up and inspire changes for the better, then work to make that a reality.

16 | CONFIDENCE

"Conflicts are bound to happen, and no one likes it. Instead of running away or passing blames, confident leaders work through whatever issues arise head-on, solve the problems, and get results."

Confidence is a critical component of leadership. It is so essential that without it, authentic leadership cannot exist. It is the basis for a leader to make a difficult decision, get team members to communicate candidly, and lead meetings with authority. Confidence comes from within; most leaders do not have it. It doesn't mean they are weak. It only implies they feel insecure or have a negative perspective about themselves and the projects they undertake.

Other leadership skills, stated in the previous chapters of this book, can be taught to a leader. However, if such a leader does not first believe in himself/herself, authentic leadership will be impossible. Teaching leadership without first building confidence would only make leadership exist in the title because getting the team will be impossible.

No one wants to work with leaders who lack confidence because they will always be viewed as incompetent and cannot be trusted. When those around you feel your confidence, among other qualities, they trust you more and become more willing to invest their time and energy to work with you to ensure that projects are successful. If you don't believe that you can lead, you will flop!

Leaders with self-confidence act and think positively about their visions and plans, and as a result, they are more likely and willing to take risks necessary to achieve the ultimate goal. They happily play their parts as leaders in confidence, dealing with daily challenges, and have a tenacious attitude. Confident leaders perform the best.

Being a confident leader enables individuals to inspire others to act quickly. It also increases team commitment. Unlike leaders who lack confidence, confident leaders are more likely to speak up and support their teams. When you are sure enough to stand up for your team members in the face of adversity and criticism, they will be committed and motivated to go above and beyond for you. They understand their team deserves better, and they are not crippled with fear of the consequences. Rather than cower in fear, they are ready to fight back.

These leaders are also known to tackle issues, manage difficult conversations effectively, and solve complex problems within their team quickly to ensure disruption is reduced. Conflicts are bound to happen, and no one likes it. Instead of running away or passing blames, confident leaders work through whatever issues arise head-on, solve the problems, and get results. Since they are confident and believe that they are doing the right thing, they comfortably engage in a difficult conversation. Rather than put off such discussions for later and hope it will somehow resolve itself, which rarely happens, they tackle it quickly and are more likely to solve team issues and reduce disruption, fueling the team's work drive.

16 | CONFIDENCE

Leaders who often find themselves second-guessing their words and decisions or feel they don't have the skills to tackle such issues end up losing trust and loyalty from their subordinates.

With confidence, delegation becomes much easier. Confident leaders are more likely to delegate tasks because they are not insecure and are never ruled by fear of the assigned team member screwing up. They do not keep tight control over functions. They let go, so team members can get the chance to take on different opportunities they might not usually have and improve their skills.

With this type of action, these leaders build trust with team members to get the job done while saving time and energy. With less control comes less work, enabling them to utilize their capacities to the fullest.

We might align confidence with a leader's intellect, such as the sentiment that confident leaders always have the correct answer. However, it isn't always so. Confident leaders know they do not have superhuman powers to know EVERYTHING, and that's why they hire a team of professionals to provide solutions, give feedback, and complement their shortcomings. These leaders do not feel insecure when their team members contribute ideas they never thought about, nor do they portray the "I am the boss" attitude to shut down opinions from subordinates. Instead, they embrace these inputs and feedback with open-mindedness, increasing teamwork, creativity, and diversity of views, creating improved results.

When a team's input and guidance are taken and put into practice, they feel valued, appreciated, and that their ideas and opinions matter, therefore trusting you more.

Having confidence as a leader also implies trying new things. These leaders are open to risks and not afraid to fail. They often try new things and change them later if they're not working. They confidently forge into the unknown, learn from potential failures, and create a more creative, dynamic work culture where teams can suggest ideas and try things without fear of repercussions.

Being a confident leader is not just great for your team but also for yourself as a leader. You feel good about yourself, become happier even in challenging situations, have better mutual respect in relationships, and become motivated to accomplish your set goals.

In most cases, confident leaders aren't born secure, so they can be built over time and improved upon.

Practical Steps

Here are some tips to guide you into becoming confident:

Recognize Your Strengths, Skills, and Talents

It would help if you spent some alone time looking inwards, knowing and reconnecting with your strengths. It will help you to stay focused on them and express yourself in them. In taking some time off to reconnect with yourself, try not to compare yourself with others; you'll end up comparing their strengths with your weaknesses, leaving you with reduced esteem.

Take Pride in Yourself

After realizing your strengths, take pride in them by appreciating who you are, how far you have come, and what you can accomplish.

It can motivate you when the going becomes tough! However, taking pride in yourself should be done with humility, not by putting others down.

Acknowledge Your Self-doubt

Everyone has self-doubt, and some situations will certainly make you doubt yourself. However, if you don't address it, it doesn't go away. One way to do this is to hold back your inner voice of self-doubt. You can also identify the situation that made you doubt yourself, work to understand where it's coming from, and resolve to tune it out entirely.

Eliminate Triggers and Embrace Catalysts

Study yourself to know what triggers insecurity and makes you feel bad about yourself. Is it the people you spend time with or places or situations? Anything that leaves you thinking you're not good enough should be eliminated.

Also, embrace things that make you feel good about yourself. Surround yourself with people who believe you're great and can do the impossible. Surround yourself with people that inspire you to be your best. Be intentional about maintaining those relationships because they'll build confidence in you and lift your perspective. You don't need to have a houseful of them. It would be best if you didn't mistake this with flatterers; avoid those at all costs.

Bounce Back from Mistakes

You are imperfect and still growing; you are bound to make mistakes. But don't let these mistakes make you feel like you don't have what it takes. Instead, it should be your learning opportunity. Stop moping over the past; it's time to move on. One wrong turn, or even a few of them, shouldn't deny you greater opportunities.

Leverage Your Self-doubt into Confidence

Whenever you're in doubt over something, put all the self-doubt aside and concentrate on what you know (knowledge), what you know how to do (capabilities), and how well you do it (competence).

Confidence separates average leaders from great leaders. It is more important than experience, knowledge, or skills. It isn't natural for everyone, but it can be built. Otherwise, you will find yourself becoming defensive when challenged or second-guessing yourself after a decision is made. No doubt, several situations may arise during any stage of the project execution that may make you feel more or less confident, but putting efforts into eliminating self-doubts will get you through those situations. Thus, confidence is worth building over time, not just for your team but also for yourself as a leader and a person. So, start to do something daily to boost your leadership confidence.

17 | SELF-AWARE

"Self-awareness helps you become more adaptable, improving your confidence and strengthening your vulnerability as you are open about your flaws, needs, and strengths."

We all have blind spots when it comes to our abilities. We often make the mistake of thinking that everything we do will always work. However, a break from those blind spots makes you more aware of yourself. Self-awareness is one of the essential capabilities that a leader should have. It is a prerequisite for other leadership skills. A leader must be aware of his/her personality before he/she can have a solid moral compass, organizational skills, and the ability to communicate clearly, among other skills.

This trait is the first step for a leader in developing emotional intelligence, which is highly valuable in leadership. Self-awareness, once created, makes a leader know his strengths and weaknesses, triggers, and motivators. Once their strength is recognized and appreciated, they put them forward and lean into those abilities while examining their vulnerabilities without self-judgment, empowering themselves to work on them. Self-awareness also enables them to monitor their emotions and reactions. It allows them to take a deeper look at why they feel a certain way and how those feelings turn into responses to any given situation.

In addition to being aware of your emotions, self-awareness includes knowing how to react to others. Self-awareness helps you become more adaptable, improving your confidence and strengthening your vulnerability as you are open about your flaws, needs, and strengths.

When your self-awareness abilities are improved, you will be perceptively in tune with yourself and your emotions, becoming more empathetic because of the heightened emotional intelligence that comes with this trait. Once we understand ourselves, we understand and appreciate others better.

In being more conscious of their actions, emotions, and biases, these leaders also have sound situational awareness, knowing and having control over when and how to react while guiding those around them to develop their self-knowledge and success. Having a clear understanding of their emotions, abilities, and limitations enables these leaders to communicate and build stronger relationships effectively.

Self-awareness improves their sensitivity to know when they've offended a team member. They are pretty aware of their impacts on their team members.

Self-awareness keeps leaders attuned and focused on why they wanted to become leaders in the first place. Thus, they become efficient and deliberate in staying on task. It also improves their confidence as they discover and live the impact they want to have on their team members. These leaders are humble enough to acknowledge that humans are filled with imperfection, thus not knowing everything. Since they've taken cognizance of their strengths, weaknesses, and hidden biases and are accountable for them, they consistently ask for feedback and look for other ways to improve. With them being self-aware, they value continuous learning and growth, investing in a professional development program.

In addition to being humble and open to feedback, self-aware leaders constantly make a conscious effort to forgive themselves and those around them whenever they are able. They recognize that we don't live in a perfect world, and no one's perfect.

By becoming more self-aware, these leaders gain the trust, respect, and understanding of their team members. They create a work culture that promotes learning and development, an environment with regular check-ins and self-reflection. Team members can openly put their tensions on the table to be addressed without feeling hurt or intimidated.

Self-awareness also helps leaders create a positive impact while on the job. There is a low chance of experiencing internal conflict and a high probability of meeting project goals and achieving results.

Self-awareness is a conscious effort. It takes work and willingness to recognize and understand who you are, your emotions, feelings, etc., in line with who others are. Learning to be aware of yourself isn't an easy task, but mastering and practicing it leads to improvement and makes one a much more effective leader.

A simple way to start being aware is to engage in personality assessments. It includes getting an unbiased and professional opinion about your strengths and limitations, how you function, what drives you, etc.

While assessing yourself, stay focused. Cut out all distractions such as being carried away with beeps and dings from social media, emails, etc. You are trying to make connections with yourself, so train yourself to focus for long periods.

Be Mindful of Your Strengths and Weaknesses

Engaging in personal assessment helps you be aware of your strengths and limitations, and you can work from that space. Being aware of these implies that you know when to ask for help or work towards improvement on your own. Identifying your emotions will help you understand your emotional triggers and work on them when communicating with others. For instance, when faced with a tough challenge, you might either take a deep breath or take a stroll.

Keep an Open Mind

Avoid being arrogant, accept feedback, and work on your limitations. Although being open-minded can make you look vulnerable, it improves your weaknesses. The more relaxed you are to team members, the more you garner respect, loyalty, and understanding from them.

Be Curious About Knowing People

When you can control your emotional being, you tend to be in harmony with others' emotions. You can't regulate your emotions in response to other's reactions if you aren't curious about them and all they have to offer.

Set Boundaries

Knowing your emotions will allow you to set firm boundaries in place to maintain not just your integrity but the project plans, execution of your goals, and the work you put into those goals and plans. It will enable you to politely say no when you need to and keep you disciplined and focused.

Being self-aware will enable you to trust your instincts and take risks associated with them. Your instincts will tell you what to do next.

Practical Steps

Here are a few self-awareness activities that can help increase self-awareness and allow you to make positive changes in your behavior while also increasing your self-confidence.

Simple Breathing Exercise:

- Find a quiet place void of any distractions or disturbances.

- Sit in a chair or, preferably, on the floor.

- Keep your back and neck straight.

- Stay focused on the present moment. If you have trouble staying focused, develop an awareness of your breath by focusing on the rising and falling of your belly and the feeling of air moving in and out of your body as you breathe.

- Now, observe every thought that comes; don't ignore them but make a note of them, using your breath as an anchor. Try not to think about the past or future. After acknowledging them, let them go as they come.

- Don't go too hard on yourself; self-awareness doesn't come easily and naturally. So, strive for a minute or more initially and work your way up to more extended periods.

Grounding Technique:

Another excellent tool for developing self-awareness is Grounding Techniques. They help you connect with the earth, calm your nerves, and bring your focus into the present.

- Sit on a comfortable chair with your eyes shut.
- Let your feet touch the floor.
- Start breathing in and out to the count of three.
- Next, divert your focus to your body; notice how you feel at your legs, feet, and body in general. Also, observe how your back feels against the chair, the fabric's texture, and how the seat feels.
- Now, imagine pushing your feet into the ground. Visualize your energy draining down from your mind and out through your feet into the ground.
- As you picture this, you will realize how heavy each part of your body feels. It will help you relax your muscles and get a clear recognition of your overall personality.

Keep a journal because you are likely to:

- Discover your passions, strengths, interests, and talents.
- Know how you feel when you are doing what you like.
- Understand your thoughts and beliefs, emotions, and sources of motivation.
- Recognize other people and how they view you and your actions.

CONCLUSION

Irrespective of your title, position, skills, and experience, these undeniable traits guarantee tremendous success, not just in executing projects but in creating a long-lasting impact on the team you work with. You will love the feeling when everyone loves working with you. Since it's a feeling you will love, put in the effort to practice each skill's steps because the result is worth it!

ABOUT THE AUTHOR

Nicole Sanchez has always been ambitious, motivated, and enthusiastic about her work, as well as enthusiastic about sharing her energy with others. She spent almost 17 years at Wells Fargo in sales and leadership before finding her true calling in construction.

After the banking industry, she joined one of the top engineering firms in Southern California and quickly rose through the ranks. Her first promotion put her into the role of VP of Sales. Her performance and ability to lead propelled her into her next promotion as VP of Operations.

Never content to settle, Nicole focuses on creating content to help inspire and influence others. She is a firm believer that success is not just about what we accomplish in life but helping and inspiring others to accomplish extraordinary things as well. She hosts a successful podcast, called "The Construction Influencer," where she sits down with some of the top leaders in construction to talk about all things #Leadership and what it takes to build and operate a successful company.

Looking towards the future, Nicole wants to spend even more of her energy inspiring others. Regardless of where you came from, how many mistakes you might have made in life, or how many times you may have failed, get up, dust yourself off, and try again. Whatever you do, don't ever give up on your dreams, and most importantly, never give up on yourself.

Success is not just about what we accomplish in life, but helping and inspiring others to accomplish extraordinary things as well.

www.ingramcontent.com/pod-product-compliance
Lightning Source LLC
Chambersburg PA
CBHW070649220526
45466CB00001B/367